A SOCK IS BORN

WRITTEN & ILLUSTRATED BY EMILY C. CÔTÉ

A SOCK IS BORN

1405 SW 6th Avenue • Ocala, Florida 34471 • Phone 352-622-1825 • Fax 352-622-1875
Website: www.atlantic-pub.com • Email: sales@atlantic-pub.com
SAN Number: 268-1250

Library of Congress Control Number: 2020907630

Printed in the United States

PROJECT MANAGER: Kassandra White
INTERIOR LAYOUT AND JACKET DESIGN: Nicole Sturk

FOR MY FAMILY, WHO ALWAYS ENCOURAGES THE ASKING OF GOOD QUESTIONS.

AND FOR ALL THE OTHERS WHO DARE TO ASK.

I WANT TO TELL YOU
A VERY SPECIAL
STORY.

IT'S A STORY YOU
MAY NOT HAVE
HEARD BEFORE.

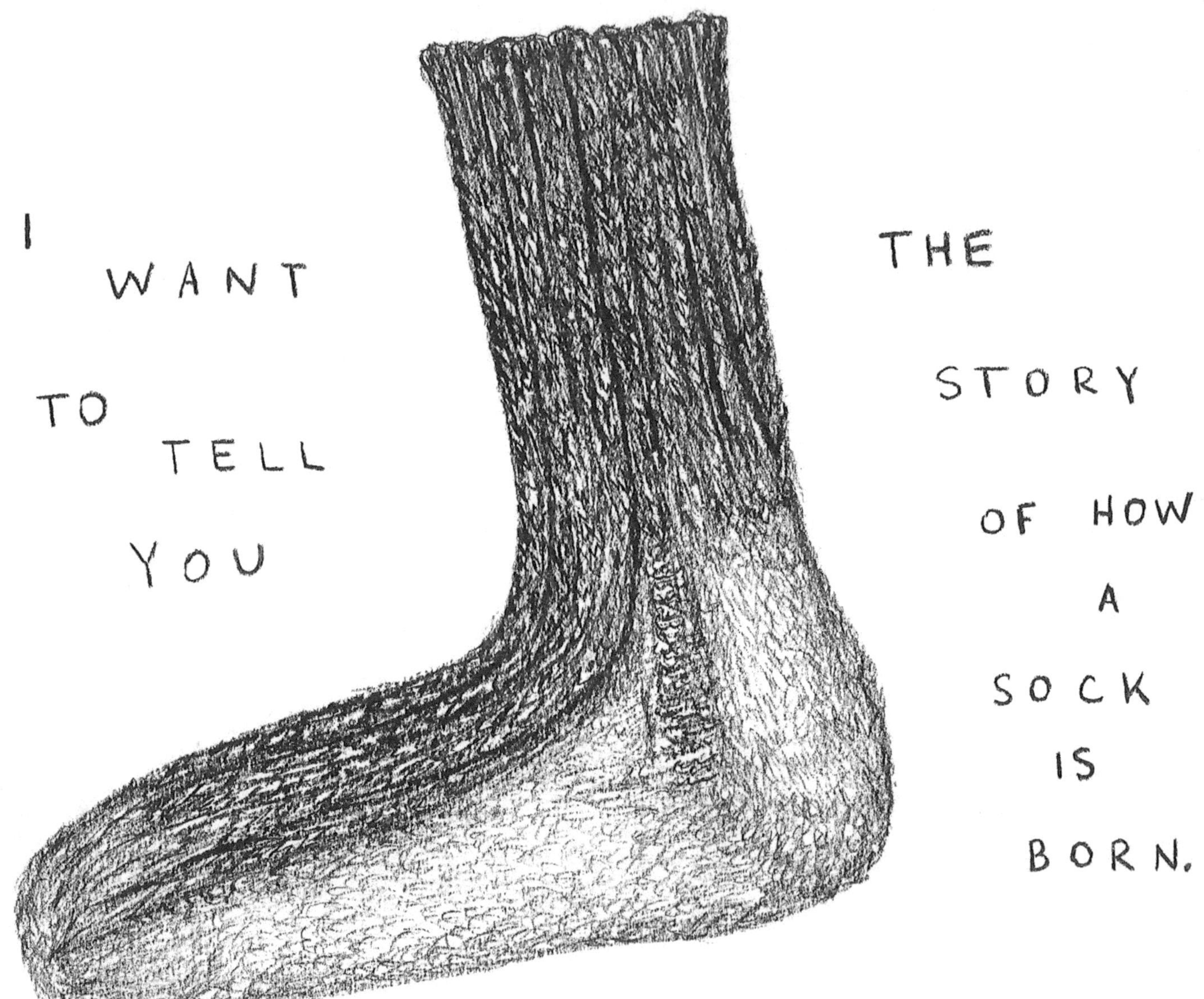
I WANT TO TELL YOU
THE STORY OF HOW A SOCK IS BORN.

IN OUR WORLD, THERE ARE MANY DIFFERENT KINDS OF SOCKS —

THERE ARE SOCKS WITH MANY DIFFERENT PATTERNS,

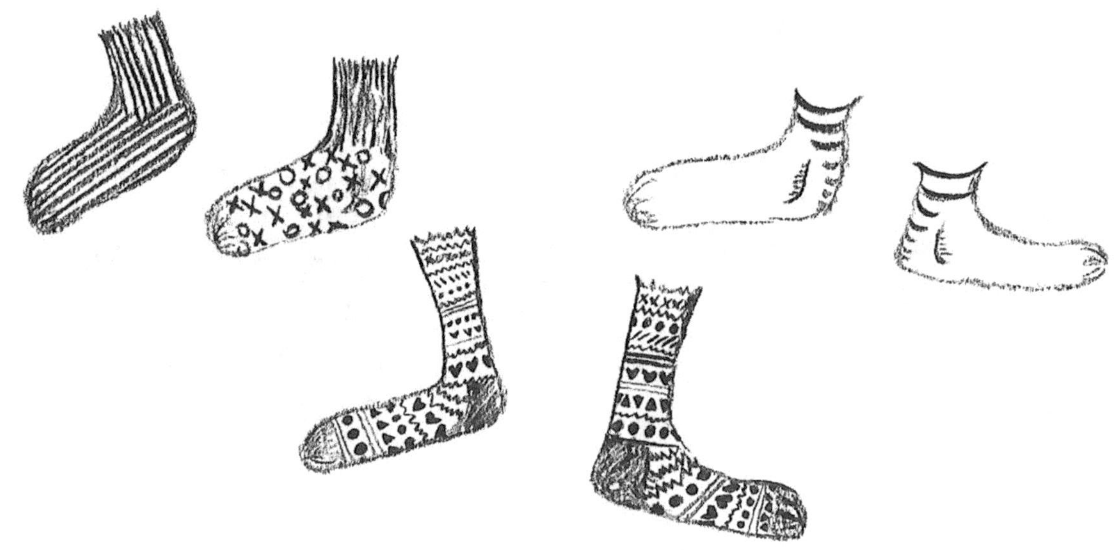

MADE OF MANY DIFFERENT THINGS.

BUT THE SOCK WE WILL MEET TODAY IS MADE OF

WOOL...

FROM A SHEEP!
HERE IS THE SHEEP,
SPENDING TIME
WITH HER
FRIENDS
IN A
LOVELY
MEADOW.

SHE GROWS HER FLEECE ALL YEAR LIKE A BUILT-IN SWEATER, UNTIL SPRING...

WHEN IT'S TIME FOR
A BIG HAIRCUT!

NOW, DURING THE SUMMER
SHE WON'T GET TOO HOT.
WE WILL NOW FOLLOW THAT PILE OF WOOL
TO THE NEXT PAGE!

FRESH FROM THE SHEEP, THE WOOL HAS SOME DIRT AND BITS OF PLANTS IN IT.

WE'LL GIVE IT A GOOD BATH TO WASH THOSE OUT.

SHEEP ALSO HAVE A
SPECIAL OIL ON THEIR SKIN,
CALLED LANOLIN, WHICH
STAYS IN THEIR WOOL.
WE'LL KEEP THAT,
BECAUSE IT WILL COME
IN HANDY FOR THE
MAKING OF OUR
SOCK.

NOW, IT IS TIME TO COMB THE WOOL.

THE WOOL IS VERY CURLY,

AND COMBING IT HELPS LOOSEN THE CURLS.

COMBING ALSO HELPS TAKE ANY SMALL NUBBY BITS OUT OF THE WOOL-

AND ALIGNS THE FIBERS TOGETHER.

ALL OF THESE THINGS WILL BE IMPORTANT FOR THE NEXT STEP.

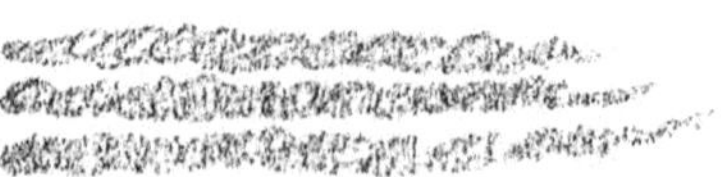

TOOLS FOR COMBING WOOL

(THIS IS ALSO CALLED CARDING):

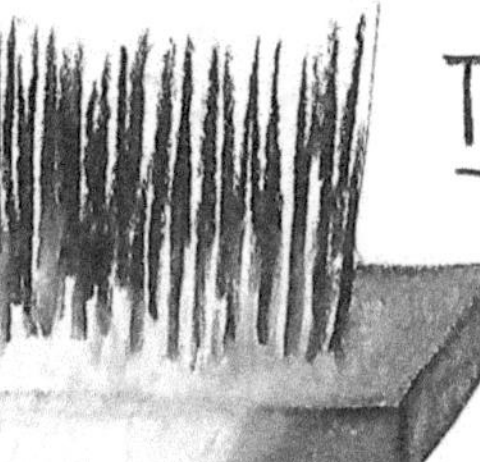

THE HECKLE.

THE SPIKES ON THE HECKLE ARE VERY STRONG AND SHARP, SO WE'LL NEED TO WATCH OUR FINGERS!

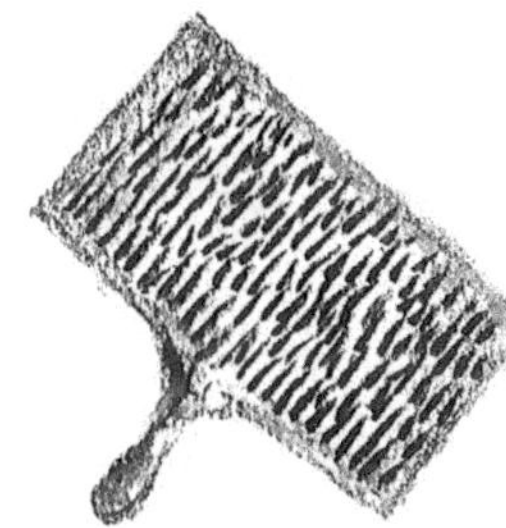

HAND CARDERS.

HAND CARDERS ARE LIKE BIG DOG-COMBS.

NOW, IT'S TIME TO MAKE THE YARN!

THIS IS CALLED SPINNING.

SPINNING IS WHAT HAPPENS WHEN FIBER IS TWISTED. WHEN WE twist THE FIBER ENOUGH, IT TRANSFORMS FROM FLUFF INTO A STRONG THREAD.

YOU CAN TRY THIS YOURSELF WITH A COTTON BALL.

SPREAD OUT THE FLUFF, THEN HOLD ONE END WITH EACH HAND

HERE ARE THE TOOLS WE USE TO MAKE YARN.

THE SPINDLE!

USING A SPINDLE IS JUST LIKE USING YOUR HANDS TO TWIST THE COTTON BALL, EXCEPT THE SPINDLE HAS ROOM TO STORE THE YARN ONCE IT'S MADE.

THE SPINNING WHEEL USES A FOOT PEDAL, WHICH MAKES THE BIG WHEEL SPIN. WHEN THE WHEEL SPINS, IT TRANSFERS THE SPINNING MOTION TO THE FIBER, TWISTING THE FIBER AS YOU HOLD IT.

WOW, WE'RE ALMOST THERE!

WHEN THE YARN IS MADE,
IT'S TIME TO KNIT.

TO KNIT, YOU NEED AT LEAST TWO NEEDLES.

THEY OFTEN LOOK LIKE THIS:

BUT FOR A SOCK, WE WILL NEED FOUR KNITTING NEEDLES, THAT EACH HAVE TWO POINTY ENDS.

HERE ARE THE STITCHES WE'LL USE TO MAKE OUR SOCK.

THE KNIT STITCH:

THE PURL STITCH:

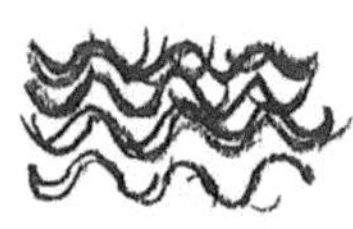

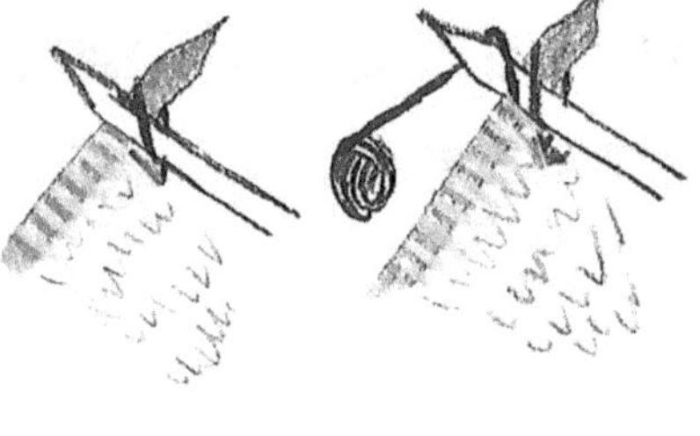

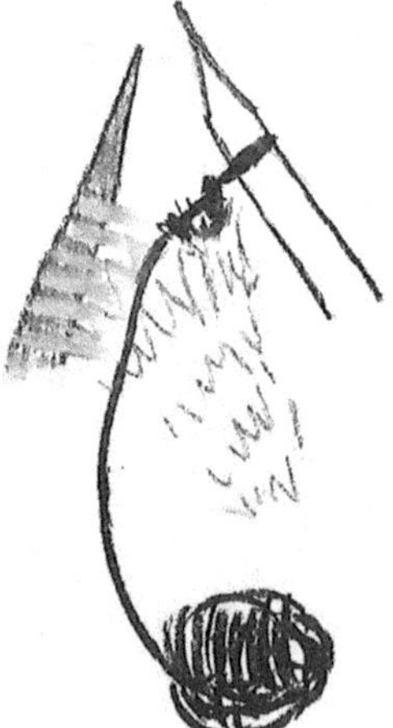

THE RIB STITCH:

KNIT, PURL, KNIT, PURL.

FIRST, WE WILL KNIT THE ANKLE OF THE SOCK USING THE RIB STITCH.

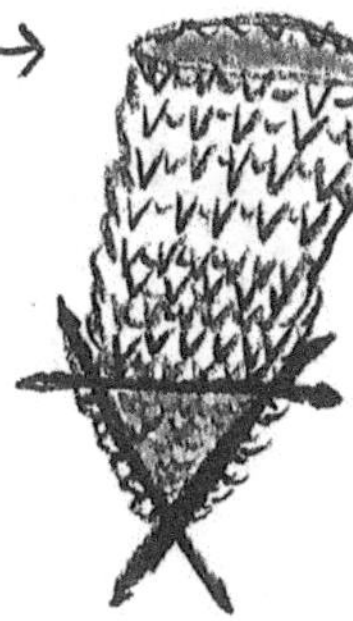

KNIT,
PURL,
KNIT,
PURL.

THEN, WE'LL "TURN THE HEEL"– WHICH REQUIRES ADDING SOME STITCHES, TAKING SOME AWAY, AND USING JUST A LITTLE BIT OF MAGIC.

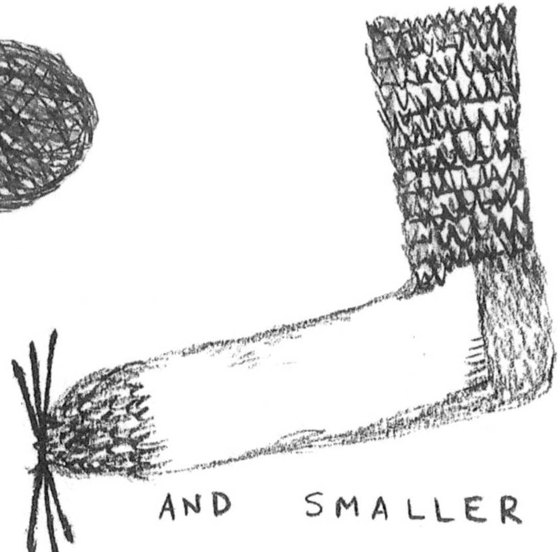

AFTER THAT, WE WILL KNIT THE FOOT, AND FINALLY, WE'LL MAKE IT SMALLER AND SMALLER TO SHAPE THE PLACE WHERE THE TOES WILL GO.

ALL IN ALL,
IT WILL TAKE
SIX TO EIGHT
HOURS TO
KNIT ONE SOCK!

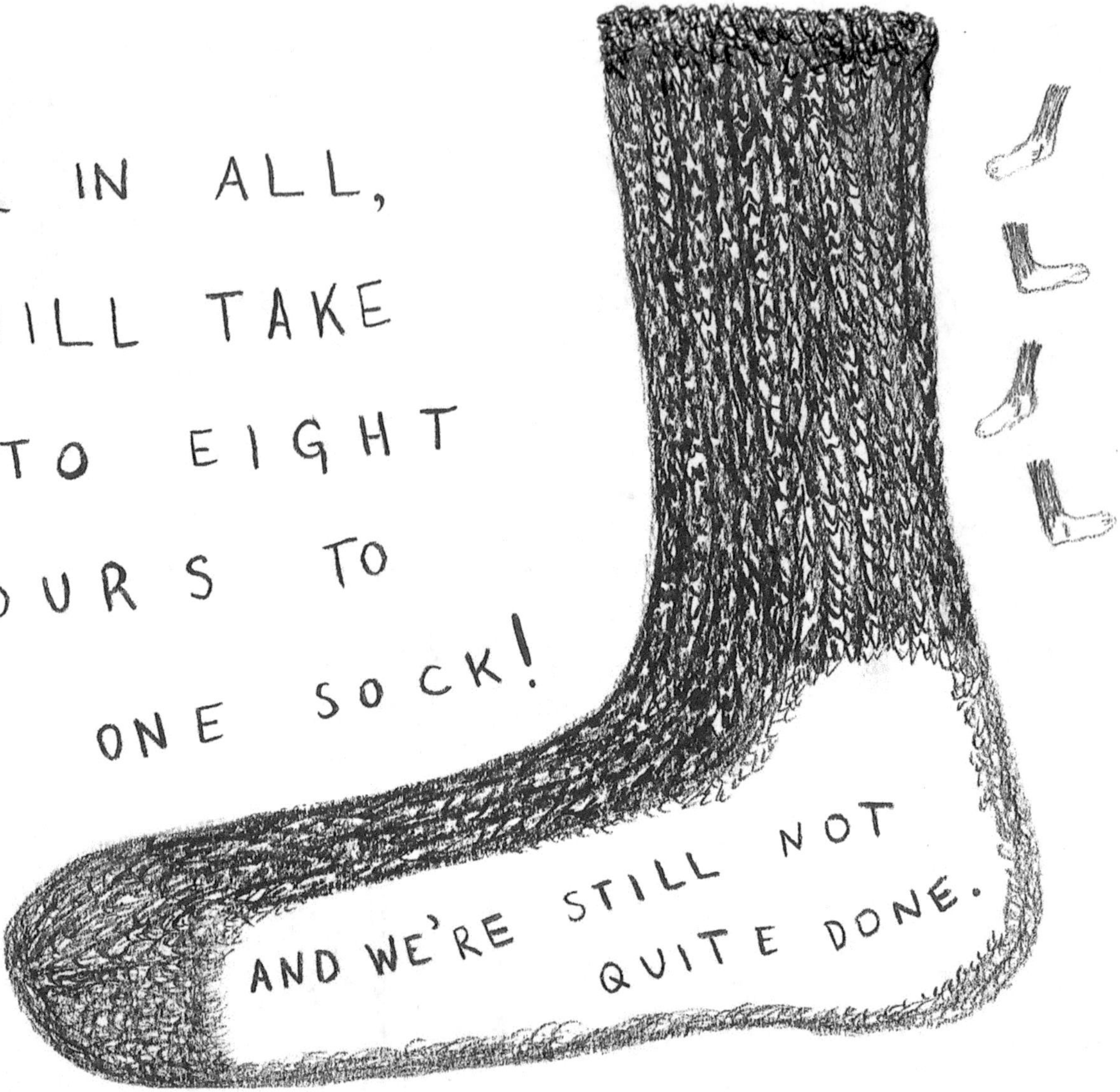

AND WE'RE STILL NOT
QUITE DONE.

OF COURSE, THE ONE SOCK NEEDS A FRIEND–

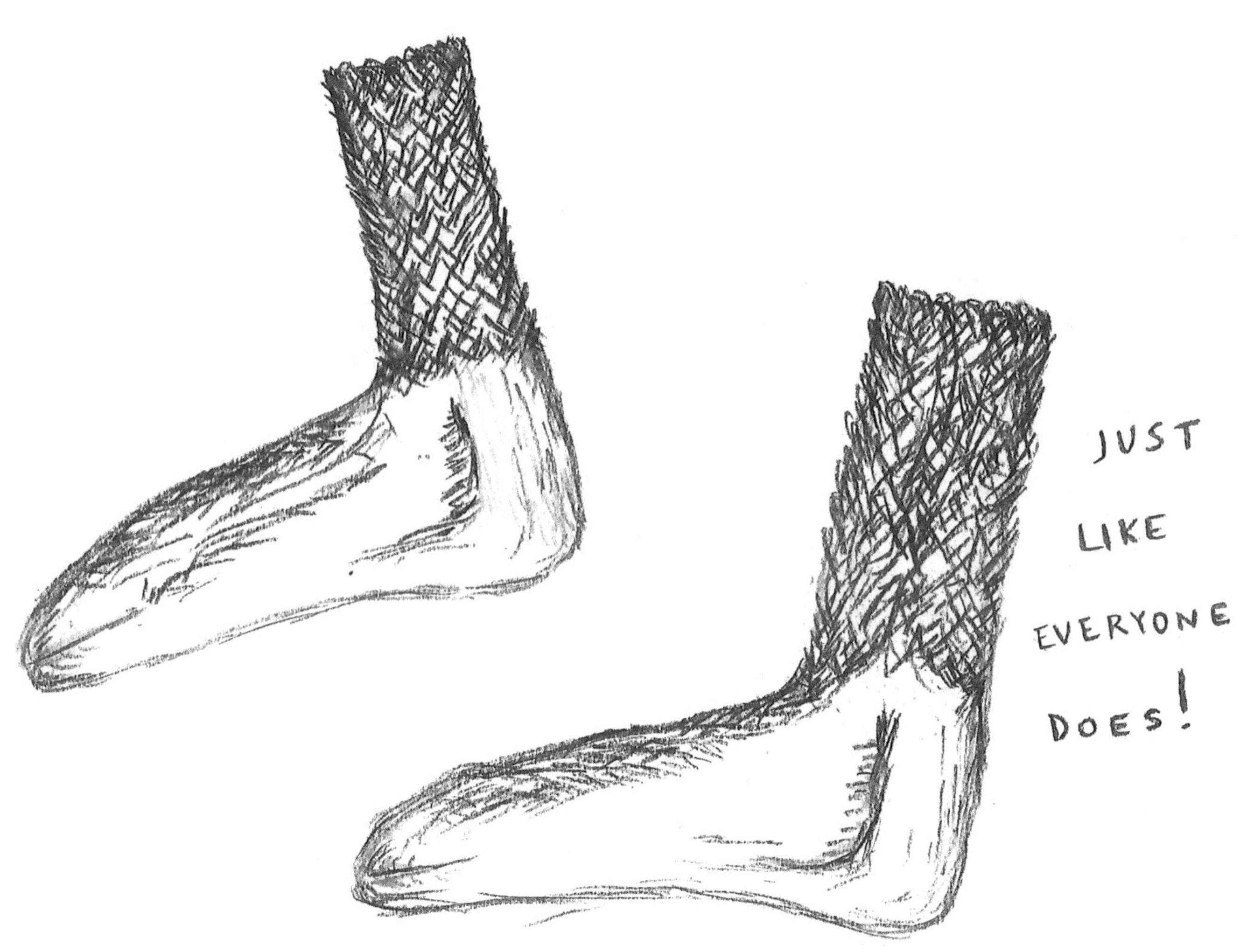

AFTER BOTH SOCKS ARE KNIT, THEY'LL GET A QUICK BATH AND RELAX FOR A BIT.

WHEN THEY COME OUT, THE STITCHES WILL BE SOFT AND RELAXED, AND THEY'LL BE IN THE RIGHT SHAPE.

ADDING ESSENTIAL OILS TO THEIR BATH WILL MAKE THEM SMELL NICE.

WHAT A JOURNEY WE'VE TAKEN!

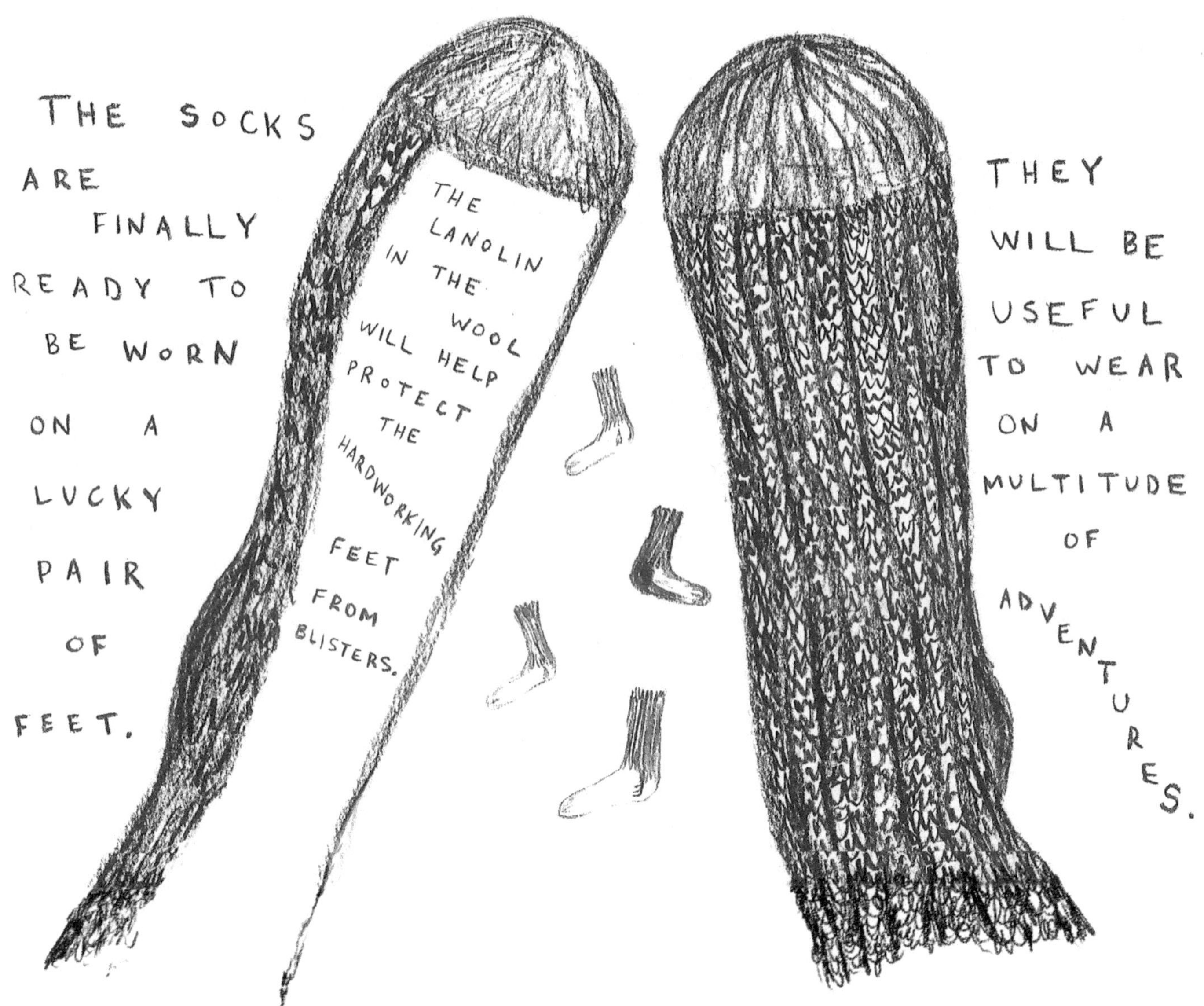

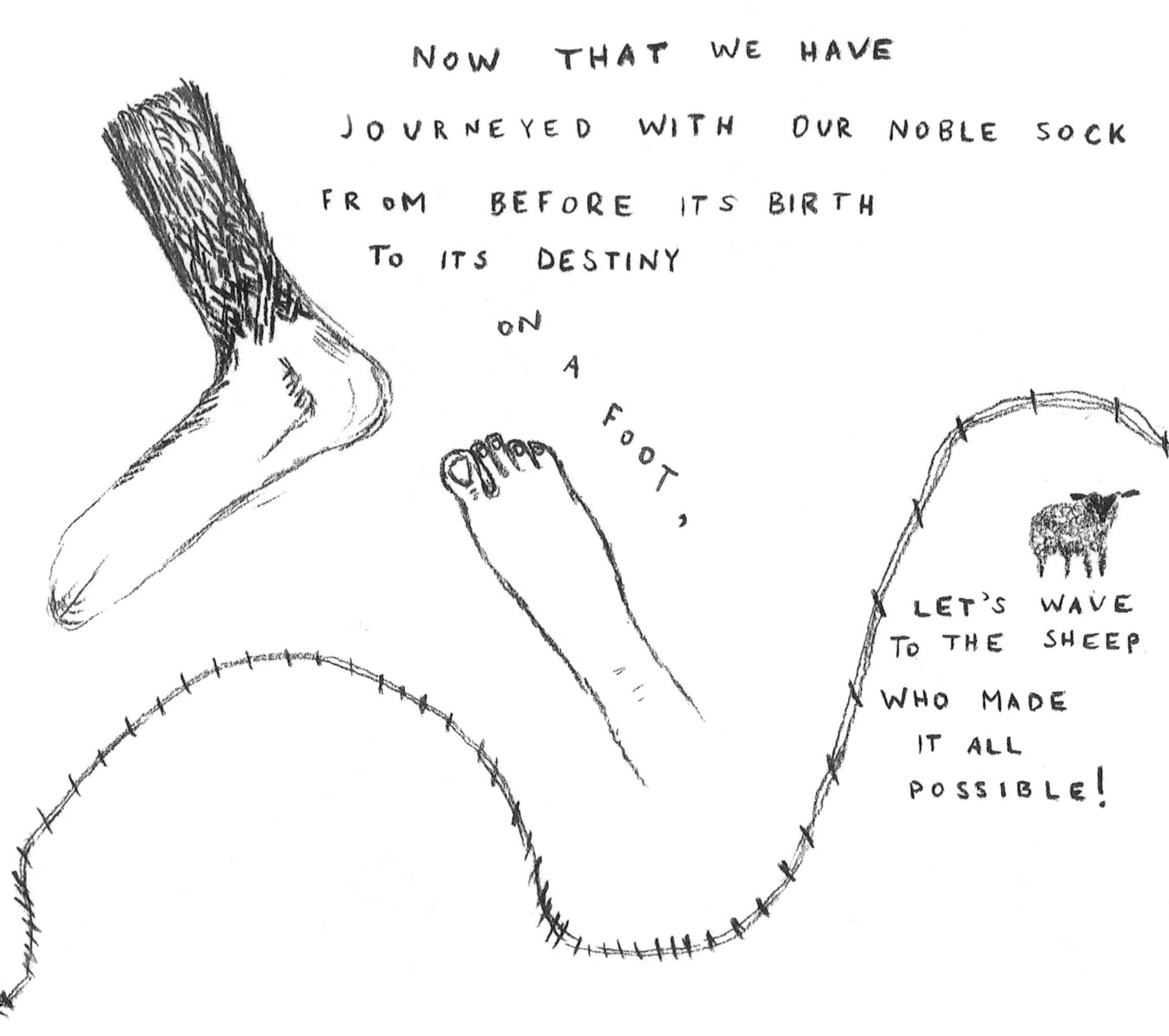
NOW THAT WE HAVE
JOURNEYED WITH OUR NOBLE SOCK
FROM BEFORE ITS BIRTH
TO ITS DESTINY
ON A FOOT,
LET'S WAVE TO THE SHEEP
WHO MADE IT ALL POSSIBLE!

FURTHER READING

KNITTING WITHOUT TEARS BY ELIZABETH ZIMMERMANN: WRITTEN BY THE COOLEST KNITTER IN THE WORLD. THIS BOOK TAUGHT ME HOW TO KNIT SOCKS.

KIDS KNITTING BY MELANIE FALICK: THE BEST INTRODUCTION TO KNITTING FOR YOUNG PEOPLE. THIS BOOK TAUGHT ME HOW TO BEGIN KNITTING!

RESPECT THE SPINDLE BY ABBY FRANQUEMONT: THE BEST BOOK FOR UNDERSTANDING SPINNING FROM THE INSIDE OUT, AND FOR LEARNING HOW TO USE A SPINDLE, WHICH IS THE MOST ACCESSIBLE WAY TO MAKE YARN.

AND MY OWN WEBSITE, WWW.REMNANTTRADINGCOMPANY.COM, WHERE YOU CAN LEARN ABOUT UPCOMING CLASSES ON A VARIETY OF FIBER ARTS TOPICS, OR EVEN GET YOUR OWN PAIR OF THE SOCKS FROM THIS BOOK!

About the Author

Emily C. Côté is a fiber and mixed-media artist, who loves making things, building campfires, and asking questions about how to live in harmony with the earth. After making friends with some alpaca farmers in 2014, she started making her own yarn, which led to a series of fortunate events, like spending time on all sorts of farms, learning to cultivate environmental sustainability, and teaching traditional fiber craft to adults and children. Her business, Remnant Trading Company (www.remnanttradingcompany.com), offers handmade solutions for low-waste homes. She lives in the Upper Peninsula of Michigan and Illinois. This is her first book.

www.ingramcontent.com/pod-product-compliance
Lightning Source LLC
LaVergne TN
LVHW081302100826
845148LV00005B/947

* 9 7 8 1 6 2 0 2 3 7 8 2 3 *